WHAT TRAVELS WITH US

WHAT TRAVELS
WITH US

—POEMS—

DARNELL ARNOULT

LOUISIANA STATE UNIVERSITY PRESS *Baton Rouge*

Designer: Melanie O'Quinn Samaha
Typeface: Garamond 3
Printer and binder: Edwards Brothers, Inc.

LIBRARY OF CONGRESS CATALOGING-IN-PUBLICATION DATA

Arnoult, Darnell, 1955–
    What travels with us : poems / Darnell Arnoult.
      p. cm.
    ISBN 0-8071-2989-5 (pbk. : alk. paper)
    I. Title.
PS3601.R586W47   2005
811'.6—dc22

                                        2005015541

Grateful acknowledgment is made to the editors of the following
publications, in which the poems listed first appeared, sometimes in a
slightly different form: *Asheville Poetry Review,* "Arthur and Lilly: Hotel
Roanoke"; *Brightleaf: A Southern Review of Books,* "Photograph in the
Hall"; *Frontage Road,* "Labor of Leaving" and "Ignorance in High Places";
Nantahala Review, "Home," "House Party," "Some in Pieces," and
"Liberty Heights Pool" (under the title "Clear Water"); *Now and Then
Magazine,* "Immersion"; *Sandhills Review,* "Angels"; *Southern Cultures,*
"Learning Strategy at English Field."

For Chad and Beth
and in memory of
Maude and Tommy

Now then rise early in the morning
with the servants of your lord
who came with you,
and start early in the morning,
and depart as soon as you have light.

I SAMUEL 29:10

CONTENTS

ACKNOWLEDGMENTS

I wish to thank Katheryn Stripling Byer, Lee Smith, Lucinda McKethan, and John Easterly for their time, patience, and dedicated help with the shaping of this manuscript. Thanks to Spencer Wood for his careful editing and gracious communication and to everyone at LSU Press who had a hand in the making and promoting of this book. Thanks also to Parks Lanier, founding director of the Selu Writers Retreat at Radford University, where many of these poems were written, and to the Selu sisters, particularly Tamara Baxter, Heidi Hartwiger, and Isabel Zuber. Thank you to the Roger Florish Writers Group, particularly Virginia Boyd, Pamela Duncan, and Lynn York, and to the Grey Mules Writers Circle. Thank you Dixie Childress, Michael Chitwood, Ruthie Ervin, Georgann Eubanks, Jaki Shelton Green, Iris Tillman Hill, Michael McFee, Tom Rankin, Shelby Stevenson, Tom Lisk, and Dana Wildsmith. Thanks to my family for teaching me the importance of a good story and then for giving me lots of stories to work with. Most importantly, I am grateful for and to my children, Chad and Beth Stone, who have encouraged me these many years, and my loving husband, William Brock, who has, from the day we met, supported my desire to write—sometimes to the point of sacrifice. "Shorts Creek" is for Phyllis Grayson, Tracy and Jillian Mays, "Some in Pieces" and "Oral History" are for Louise and Gerald Burch, "Learning Strategy at English Field" is for Carol Stone, "Response" is for Chad and Beth Stone, and "Outrageous Love" is for William Brock.

WHAT TRAVELS WITH US

ELIJAH'S PLACE

Elijah Whitlock lived
in a little white house—
a box that became a barn,
and by my time a shed.

One oiled paper window
next to a flint rock chimney.
Grease lamps
rendered evening light.

White oak shingles cut
with a froe and maul
layered in the old
of the moon
kept water out.

To roof in the new
of the moon
was apt to
cause shingles to curl.

A leather latch-string
was out the latch hole
if a visitor was welcome.

No latch-leather—
no welcome.

How long
did I wait for
him to come love me? Lord!
I was starving! But hard as his
heart was

it was
food to me. Why
I had to bite my way
to that poor blinded and bleeding
thing. A

demon
I was. Must have
smelled the blood. On some nights
between cold sheets and closed eyes I'd
feel the

dark soft
ringlets, as if
his head already lay
on that pillow there waiting for
my love

to touch.
I'd feel that man's
skin beneath my hands, his
curls sliding between my fingers.
My hands

traveling
his neck, his chest,
his belly. Trace and taste
sweet bites of ribs, of tender thigh,
morsel

of neck
meat. Must have cast
a mighty spell on him
gobbling him up like that in dreams.
He came

to me
on a Sunday.
The mountains moved closer.
I heard a whippoorwill at noon.
He knocked.

I knew
it was him and
there he stood. Said he was
eaten up by melancholy.
Eaten

by a
sorrow. Me on
his mind all the time. He
didn't show his heart to any
body.

Truly
I have married
meat and bread. As sure as
this banquet passes my lips, love
is food.

REVIVAL

Preacher Chilton preached
hollow to hollow
ridge to ridge
brush arbor to brush arbor
preacher stand to preacher stand
till Calloway.
Then it was sip after sip
of a little brandy drip
to purge his load
soul for soul.
When the last penitent
slid from his mind
he stood and said
The Lord shall preserve
thy going out and thy coming in
from this time forth
and even for evermore.
A tall man, he mounted
his sorrel mare smooth
as wind
and looked for road.

BOARDING HOUSE

Gracie came from Richmond
to teach.
Charlie rode a black Percheron
stallion
from Alumine
to court the teacher.

Pearly Rakes complained
that on long winter nights
Gracie and Charlie
kept the parlor lamp
burning too long,
burning up her kerosene.

Pearly claimed
she courted and married
the same man twice
and never burned up
nearly so much.

Charlie scratched his head.
Told Pearly,
*You musta done most of
your courting in the dark.*

Gracie got herself killed
working an ambulance
somewhere in France.
Charlie was blasted in two
at Chateau-Turney something.

Come Armistice Day,
Pearly always complains,
*After all that kerosene,
they never married.
Not even once.*

When I was a boy
sharp-looking government men
poured corn liquor on
the dusty road in front of
a bunch of folks down
at my Grandpa Burch's store.
They said they was bound
to set us dumb hillbillies
a good example.
Later, my uncles—Eslie
and Autho—catched
the runoff in Mason jars.
Then, dust settled, they
sold the top for cold hard cash.
But that's ignorant
mountain men for you, aint it?
They couldn't eat examples.

I snip these stubborn brown buttons
from your old blue shirt, faded and worn
slick, and sew them on my new green dress
made by the labor of a dissatisfied mind.
Every stitch a prayer for redemption.
Every bend of my wrist a heart's turn.

You left me alone in my silence, chose to turn
from me when I needed more than these buttons
to resew or your supper to reheat. There's no redemption
in work alone. Labor is your church, but my faith is worn
weak from unrewarded effort and your sameness of mind.
My reward is in the darts and tucks of this traveling dress.

Green stands for new life, so I'm giving myself a green dress
that dances across my lap as I turn
up the hem to hit the fat of my calf. I'm of a mind
to go shorter, but cautious. I push thread through these buttons
that you touched every day, buttons from a shirt worn
thin as tissue for lack of a better. Who would've thought redemption

could come from a simple bolt of cloth? Redemption
sold at Joyce's Mercantile for twenty-five cents a yard. A dress
be the liberator of a heart broken and childless, a heart as worn
as any shirt, or step, or stone. Guilt whispers to me. *Turn
back to the tiger lilies outside your window.* Like your buttons,
they stand out against a blanket of green, against my first mind

and my body, but not my will. I am of a second mind
now—healed from your breath at my chin. There's no redemption
in loss, no salvation in unceasing toil. I wake up each morning to buttons
moved from one shirt to another, one faded color to another. This dress—
my history changes with it, praise God. The green won't fade and turn
to thin film over my hips. It won't be worn

to thin tinted glass and show the tear in my worn
thinner slip beneath. It will stay rich, courting a mind

thirsty with questions. I need to turn
thoughts to bricks, to turn this bright redemption
into a tar-paved road out of this place. All here stops with this dress.
Every stitch marks a step to some new place. Stitches and buttons.

Steps and stones. These buttons remind me that you know nothing of redemption—
stuck in a dulled mind. Don't bother to call it sorrow. You won't lay eyes on this dress.
I'm gone with the coming light, step by step, turn by turn, button by sweet button.

SPRINGHOUSE

Buck Waller saw a
surveyor marking boundaries
at daybreak. Made Buck
right curious. Come next year ole
Buck jumped to a mill whistle.

Same surveyor begged
a cool drink from Ma at the
springhouse. Then they married.

Fore long he got hired
to drive sixteen penny nails
ground to roof. Retired fixing looms.

Quilters and planters,
milkers and miners, all got
baptized in streams of
eternal cotton spinning
thin and breakneck into yards
and yards of Jacquard white road.

Ma, she spun and spun
till she spun herself white.
She spun herself plumb fuzzy,
a dust mote on the mill floor.
Come one day, she floated off.

VOICE

Rockrun Road circles
the black Baptists' singing like
a dark gray halo.

MATTIE CLAY

August 1959
I stood before the
medicine chest
and thought how I
should be an actress.
Dew filmed my body.
My eyes were blue
sapphires. Stella in
Streetcar Named Desire.

But the thought came to me.

Instead, I went
to bed
beside my husband
and heard his sleep.

I have given birth
to five children
and bought new dresses
for each of their weddings.

Now, before
this yellowed mirror,
the sultry look worn away,
in my other future
I would play the part
of some man's mother.

Would I stand
before this mirror justified?
Or would I still bend low
to pool water
against my face and neck
to wash away
last night's kisses?

SECOND SHIFT

They're running Jacquards this week.
I'm a spinner, been spinning for ten years.
Work second and my old man works first.
He tends the kids, three. Better that way
cause he's patient. I aint. Just my nature's
all. No meanness really. Just my nature.
He makes them supper and warms it up for me
when I get home. He feeds me and then we go to bed,
him so he can get up at four in the morning
and me cause I'm tired as a old radio song.
He puts his hands on me and sometimes I want it.
Sometimes I take care to pick the lint from my hair
and tip a little of Rhonda's Shalimar behind my ears
and inside my arms. But one of us is always asleep
before the love comes. Neither of us is disappointed.
Tonight I'll have fried mackerel patties
with cream potatoes and okra stewed with tomatoes.
My old man can really cook.

HOUSE PARTY

A claw
hammer talks and
a fiddle trills June Bug
music. Feet become instruments.
Soldier's
Joy. Forked Deer.
Autho's feet slip and glide
across sawdusted boards, his jump
so slight
you can't see him
carry melody on
toes. The bow draws a sad note from
fiddle
strings and Eslie
puts a plate on Autho's
snowy head. His feet stroke pine boards.
His head
scarcely moves. Soles
of his shoes pumice the
floorboards under his feet as if
boards were
strings that vibrate
tone and rhythm under
the dexterous weight of fingertips.

HOME

I liked to live in the old
kind of house.

Plenty of good
cracks in the floor.

Finish your corn bread.
Sweep the crumbs

through the cracks.

Under the old kind of house
chickens would get em

fast as they'd fall.

SOME IN PIECES

In World War Two
the oldest
of my uncles
picked up
dead bodies
dead weight
some in pieces
and threw them
onto the beds
of trucks.
His work spread
far as he could see.
When he came
home he poured
salted peanuts
into a Co-Cola
and prepared
for life
with folks
who could
never know
some things
as long
as they lived.

CLUTCHING

Clutching covers to my chin
I pray for this child
and my own youth.
Memory strobes
like a reflection
from a spinning prom-ball.

I listen for breath.
Look for the rise and fall of her chest.
Her fingers so small, her grip so tight.

These new womanly thoughts
prey on me at night.

But I have decided
to live long,
become an old old woman
who sits in a chair
in the sun
blanket over my knees
talking
to empty air.

While my trousers cling wet and heavy as past sins,
women in hats stand on the bank and pray.
Half-bodies of men in white shirts bob on the river.
Their glazed foreheads glisten in God's own sun.

Women in hats stand on the bank and pray,
singing in disjointed chorus, *Praise Jesus. Hallelujah.*
Their glazed foreheads glisten in God's own sun.
Heads fall back calling, *God in Heaven cleanse this man.*

Singing in disjointed chorus, *Praise Jesus. Hallelujah.*
Wash away his iniquity and cleanse him. Hallelujah.
Heads fall back calling, *God in Heaven cleanse this man.*
Icy fingers clamped over my face push me down into the depths.

Wash away his iniquity and cleanse him. Hallelujah.
Cleanse and sanctify, Jesus, in this holy water, God.
Icy fingers clamped over my face push me down into the depths.
They call on God and the river to wash me in the blood of the Lamb.

Cleanse and sanctify, Jesus, in this holy water, God.
Half-bodies of men in white shirts bob on the river.
They call on God and the river to wash me in the blood of the Lamb,
while my trousers cling wet and heavy as past sins.

After the old preacher rambled
and the new preacher made out
like he knew something,
shriveled white-haired women
sang all over the place
as Primitive Baptists are apt to do.
The old preacher with
the biggest ears I ever saw
lined it out for the sisters.
Amazing grace
how sweet the sound.

If it sounded good or bad
made no difference.
Their hymn finished,
nephews, all Whitlocks—
their own daddies dead—
hoisted Autho on their shoulders.

Straight-backed and fierce-looking,
they bore him away as if they were
bearing away their own nature.

Doss was a son of Eden.
Eden, North Carolina.
Brother Charlie in Virginia
didn't give him a rib,
but he gave him a leg up,
a hand, some fingers,
helped him get his foot
in the door of a towel mill,
then hosiery, finally furniture.
But they abandoned looms
and lathes for a café
that fed the bellies
of industry,
an army whose only cause
was to make a living.

Doss happened on Maudie,
just down the mountain.
They'd both left paradise
for work. He tempted her,
invited her for a spin
in his sidecar.
She stared, shocked.
He said *Now or never.*
There's no accounting for actions
taken at a crossroads.
She stood there, by the mailbox
clutching words. The wind shifted.
Blew the words away.

Doss built a log store
at Dillons Fork.
Of a Friday and Saturday night
Doss fired up a grill and his fiddle,
played Devil's music. Called the steps
in the back room they used for a dance hall.
A holyroller pulled up

logs on the hill across the road
to save souls coming out.
Customers sat and watched,
feasting on hot dogs and cheeseburgers.
Said it was closer than the theater.

Maude seldom danced.
She patted her feet to the fiery tunes.
Tilted her head to the drone and slide.
Tapped fingers on her big thighs
while her children twirled across the floor.
A jealous man, Doss would get nervous, get ideas.
Sprinkle sand at the back steps and watch
for footprints.

Doss planted two chinaberry trees
at the edge of the garden.
Shady umbrellas for courting
after marriage. A place to look back.
She'd sit with him of an evening.
They'd talk about temptation
and what it got them.

Early Sundays he'd bathe.
Strop and blade slapped and slid.
He shaved his high cheekbones
handed down to his daughters and granddaughters.
Maude said they came
from a trace of Injun's blood.
He slipped long legs into freshly pressed trousers,
pulled a newly starched band-collar shirt
over work-muscled arms and plowman's shoulders.
Suspenders. Black socks with garters. Brogans
spit polished
like he learned to do in the Army—
as if shined shoes could save you.

Maude sent the girls
each in their turn to the chinaberries.
To each girl he said *Oh, how purdy!*

The daughters loved him
slightly more than his sons.
Sons go fight their own
wars. Have their own women.

Dressed for church
he opened a wooden box,
drew out one Eucharist—
a Cuban cigar.

He took his communion
at the edge of the yard,
in one of the Adirondack chairs.
Maude and his girls gone
to Blackberry to sing hymns
and hear about damnation,
Doss remained
in the chair he built
under chinaberries he planted.
He meditated on his brick-red earth,
on apple blossoms or tart apples ready
to fall, cherries dripping like blood, pole
beans hanging heavy, corn
green and tasseled or dry and shocked.
He cogitated on honeysuckle and saw briars
overtaking the barbwire.
He pondered spring's buttercups
or summer's hollyhocks wet
with Sunday's dew.
He drank in Pentecost of fall's fire,
rapt in God's handiwork rendered from
love and labor of flesh.

A trice of grace beneath uncommon trees,
this son of Eden held service of his design.
If he had sins, it was there,
at the edge of the garden,
he repented.
Beneath the trees
he was saved.

ANGELS

I say to myself, how hard can it be?
She's just a baby herself and that boy left her
a baby to feed and diapers to wash.
What's going to happen to us?

She's just a baby herself and that boy left her.
And I'm not ready to be a grandma.
What's going to happen to us?
I'm just thirty-five, you know. She's just fifteen.

And I'm not ready to be a grandma.
Look at your tiny hands, and oh look at you stretch!
I'm just thirty-five, you know, and she's just fifteen.
Look at that. Such a pretty sight in this world.

Look at your hands, and oh look at you stretch!
I'll tell you, we better just get moving.
Look at that. Such a pretty sight in this world.
Four rows of diapers hanging on the line dancing like so many angels.

I'll tell you, we better just get moving.
A baby to feed and diapers to wash.
Four rows of diapers hanging on the line dancing like so many angels.
I say to myself, how hard can it be?

SHADE TREE

I thought to cut this
old box elder down. Disease
took it bad last year
and it don't give much shade.
But today ain't sunny,
and I'm sitting here
in the chaise lounger looking
up through what survived against
a hazy blue sky.
Night rolls over all
them wild trees
in the distance. Still forest.
These gnarled fingers used to could
make things grow.
Now most twigs break
at the touch.
Faded velvet leaves
fight for
the chance to do
what they were put here for.
See-through bug-eaten
leaves against the sky
look like lace.
The tree's too far gone
to feed itself.
Too beautiful for me
to hurry its end.
Still, the edge of night comes on.

Yesterday we staked
our freshly bleached tent and I
echoed my new name
for the sheer sweet sound of it.
Our new life made us
hungry for the blanket tide.
Younger bodies like
corporeal May ribbons danced
and swam on sand in
moonlight blurred by velum of
sea-salted mist. My
fingers lost in your blonde curls.
Now, your name is as
familiar to me as skin—
skin scarred by sorrows
and healed by satisfactions.
Some deliberate
and some unintentional.
Years of children and
grandchildren are behind us.
The sun is high and
the sand too hot to stand still.
We best get back now.
Your smooth head is turning red
without a hat just
as my eighteen-inch waist is
buried beneath lost
years of fat torpid motion
away from this pounding sea.

Captain Til Lester
kicked some engineering ass.
Two million gallons
of fire reservoir. Looked like
a Roman coliseum.

Circles in circles.
Each ring deeper toward middle.
I liked to drown there.

Buck cut a double
gainer once from the high dive.
Sliced the still blue glass
of fourteen feet like a long
slender splinter into skin.

Girls hunting summer
we searched for arrowheads
and fairystones and prayed we'd
double date come June.

I been getting postcards from Elvis.
Truly. Pictures of him as a statue
and him as a young man.
They have little messages
like *To a true fan,* which I am,
or *I love you like no one else can,*
or *Hope this card finds you well
and happy.*
All signed
Loving you,
Elvis

Then today I got chills.
One came with a picture
of his grave all covered in
pretty flowers. No message.
Postage due.
Now, do you think Elvis Presley
sent that?
It's getting so you can't tell
who's dead and who idn't

anymore.

More coffee?

THE RIDE SOUTH

Excited twelve-year-olds,
we ride south
to the all-star game.
Gloves on our laps,
hats on our heads,
words on our lips of
Sandra Palmer's budding breasts.

What are you talking about?
my mother asks
as she turns down the
volume on the radio.
A girl's eyelashes,
Kevin tells her.

What smell is that?
we ask as we drive
windows down
through the countryside.
Cow patties, my mother says.
A heavy grassy smell,
one you can live with.
Reminds me of the state fair.

House trailers mar
green pastures and woods.
I think how glad I am
my mother is afraid
of trailer fires.
I'm glad we rent a house
and I can sleep by myself.

What smell is that?
we ask as we roll on.
Chicken droppings, my mother says.
Like living near a paper mill.
You learn not to smell it.

You walk outside every day
and pretend it's not there.

Four red-capped boys
pour from the car
into the tiny store
to the drink machine
and the bathroom.
Jeffrey's fifty cents
buys us a secret.

What smell is that?
we ask as we think about
the thing in Jeff's pocket.
Horse manure, my mother says.
Sweet and strong.
Horses are so beautiful.
It hurts to know they can be so dumb.

We play a doubleheader.
Blue caps lose.
Green caps win.
What smell is that? we ask
as we get used
to our own sour bodies.
Unmistakably goat hockey, she says.
Nothing smells worse than goats.

We all stay at my house
in a dark nest of
sleeping bags and blankets.
We take turns trying it on
and think of Sandra Palmer's
naked body.
Then Kevin blows it up and pops it
like a balloon.

Now I was eleven years old.
It was night. I had watched the store
all day, made some sales, made some change,
made some fun with the regulars
who sat in the corner and yacked.
I locked the door and night trembled.
Money was counted and coins all rolled.
The money bag was zipped and locked.
Daddy had took the key with him.
I carried a Colt .45,
heavy in my hand—but I could
shoot. Daddy said to carry it
loaded on the walk home in case
someone thought to rob me. It was
all there but what change Juanita
chucked into the dang slot machine.
I'd get blamed, but she done it to
him too. He'd get the money back.
He'd gone on business to Richmond.
He'd yack about it on Thursday
with men who stayed close to keep warm
and free of their wives for a while.
He'd tell some things in front of me,
then send me to fetch something and
tell the best parts while I was gone.
The store was padlocked behind me.
I saw Grandpa's window light float
in the moonless dark across the road.
Money was in my left hand and
the Colt in my right. Leaves rustled.
I heard steps behind me. They came
faster. The old Colt was heavy.
They came at me even faster.
The Colt was heavy all right. Rustling
leaves ran at me to rob me of
a day's work. The money hit ground.
The Colt swung out at black running

night. A flash blowed out of the blue
barrel like an angel shot out
a cannon. My hand jerked somewhere
in front of me. *Boy! Boy! That you?*
I heard Grandpa shout in echoes
of fire. I had no answer but
legs pumping to that goddamn square
of light, Colt hanging in my limp
hand, my crying trapped in my throat.
It stayed trapped in me too. Til I
was an old man. Grandpa met me
near the door with a kerosene
lantern and short-barreled shotgun.
Together we walked through the dark.
Leaves broke under our feet. Lantern
light swang back and forth til one swing
of light fell on the brown money
bag and the next one fell on a
bright red blanket. Blood spread itself
over the long speckled coat of
my own good bird dog—Corabelle.
Grandpa held the light while I dug
a grave. Sixty-some years later
I dream about that money bag
on the table just shy nickels
that Juanita threw down a slot
and my daddy heading back home,
getting closer and closer with
every shovel of dirt I throwed.

Have you ever had
  delusions of grandeur?
I read all about it
in a magazine
on the coffee table
at Dr. Broadwell's office.

Have you ever thought
you were meant for
something special?
But you were afraid.
Afraid if you tried
you'd fail?
People
would think you
a fool?

You might risk
everything
only for
  delusions of grandeur.

I have.
Thought that, I mean.

ARTHUR AND LILY

HOTEL ROANOKE

Our bodies sway in
tandem. I move inside the
odor of your suit,
your Old Spice aftershave, and
your starched white dress shirt.
A lace of bourbon teases
my mind away from
the crowd and into the song
we dance to. One from
the old days. I am inside
the music with you.
I taste your neck, and you lift
my hand palm down in
yours, circle your arm farther
round the small of my
back and lower, tightening
me to you, even
now, as the music takes me
where you are. I still
float comfortably into
you, my brittle hips
figure-eighting against you
until the music
stops and you pause that extra
second, as always,
almost nothing in real time,
wrapping me in the
last phrase from the saxophone.
The next song begins.
Still inside the old music
you whisper to me.
I know the words, but I have
gotten too old to hear them.

Slender legs that don't swish when I walk,
a belly no more curved than a soup spoon,
an ass that inspires art.
Shelves of words, some with my name on the spines.
A man with a green thumb and a good heart
who knows country life and loves occupation,
who has horses to ride and thoughts to plunder.
He likes to loafer on curving back roads in a
pale yellow drop-top Fairlane on a Sunday afternoon,
even in cool weather.
Knows a joke when he hears one.
Sleeps with his hand on my breast.
Listens to Tommy Dorsey, Ralph Stanley,
Tchaikovsky and John Lee Hooker.
Knows the words to *Now or Never.*
Takes me dancing in the kitchen.
Our spins stir lace from lead-glass windows.
Rock-steps clink mismatched china from another time.
Our slow dances make the dog and cat jealous.

A sleeping porch, a porch swing,
a pantry to hold all we need.
A comfortable room each to take words in,
then chisel some away.
A yard fragrant from roses, gardenias, hollyhocks,
bearded irises, day lilies, and four o'clocks.
Rust-spotted round-backed yard chairs,
always in a circle for making music.
A black iron fence lined with white glads
An easy swung gate.
Chinaberry trees and snowy hydrangeas.
A sandbox for the grandchildren.
One we can see from the window over our sink
in the kitchen we dance in.
Swing, foxtrot, two-step, tango, flat-foot, waltz.
Long single-malt kisses, even when we are very old.

When I was three years old, I swept the floor
in my mother's shop. Pushed and pulled all colors of hair, wet
and dry, snipped and clipped, straight and curled, with my half
sized broom. In my tiny dustpan, the piles of hair smelled
of her alchemy: shampoos, rinses, solutions, lotions. I held
the leavings of women and swayed to the music their bracelets

made, chains and hoops clicking like castanets. Rings and rings of beautiful brace-
    lets—gold, silver, brass, wood, shells, polished stones—that sometimes hit the
    floor
as women slipped their hands from beneath the black plastic capes to hold
rolling papers for permanent waves or to show Mother their natural parts.
She stroked their wet hair with a sterilized rat-tailed comb, then parted their hair
    where she wanted. The smell of their coated tresses clung fast to the tips of her
    fingers until well past supper. Mother half

noticed the different hoops hit the floor, intent on her own work. I thought jewelry
    was the half of womanhood I lacked, ornamentation. Earbobs, beads, broaches.
    But I coveted the bracelets. One Saturday morning when the shop was full of
    talking heads, old Arlie Lester, who smelled of *Evening in Paris* and *Jergens Lotion*
    and who scarred Mother's starburst linoleum floor with the pencil-sharp spikes of
    her red high heels, leaned toward me as I swept. Her wet silver hair dripped blue-
    gray potion on my arm. Miss Arlie held

out a wooden bracelet. Her trembling spotted fingers, tipped in long red nails, held
    the wooden hoop from Mexico, black as night and dotted with flowers, half
    red, half white, like stars pierced by bright yellow centers. The lacquer looked wet
    as fresh paint. She slipped the cool circle over my outstretched hand. The bracelet
    slid up and over my elbow like an arm band. Would have slid again to the floor
    if I hadn't held my arm at an angle. Bits of Arlie clung to the black circle. I smelled

Evening in Paris and Jergens Lotion, what day after day had bled into and overtaken
    the smell
of lead paint and Arlie's famous trip south of the border. I held
my wrist close to take it all in—the rite of women—then spun across the starburst
    floor,

my head back and my arms extended, in some exotic dance of celebration. I spun half
way round the shop, almost falling in my excitement. I brandished the flowered bracelet
and looked for Mother's permission. "I have so many," Arlie said. Today a soapy wet

cloth reveals the still-bright flowers against the scuffed remains of the lacquer-wet
background I wipe free of dust and attic mold. Rescued from the musty smell
of old junk in a pasteboard box. Thirty years later, the bracelet
looks so small, my womanhood so different from the memory of women held
hostage to glamour. My mother, trained to lead the mousy and plain, half
knowing their enemy, marching across the red and turquoise speckled linoleum floor

from sink to mirror, mirror to dryer, dryer to mirror, wet hair exuding the smell
of pink cream rinse, permanent wave solution or peroxide. Beauty held together by
    half
moon waves and pin curls, while sparkling bracelets dropped like tears on my newly
    swept floor.

PATH UP FROM
THE GARDEN

Granny sways
side to side
in her cotton
dress, hips huge
below the tie
of her apron.
But not
as huge
as Mrs. Stovall.
My granny
moves inside
her clothes
toward the tomatoes.
Fresh red tomato
sandwiches for lunch
on Sunbeam Bread
with mayonnaise
and black pepper,
a hidden Co-Cola
saved just for me.
Granny shifts
side to side
her breasts
long and flat
swinging slightly
across her front.
She moves toward me
and away from
the tilled land
as if she might
sway slowly
past me
over my head
and gone
tomatoes in her
hands.

Becky, my unsteady conscript, and I sneak through serpentine and tangled undertow
still spiked by last year's brittle bean poles and corn stalks. Our eyes scan the earth
for snakes. Standing on two stacked cinder blocks, I unlatch the henhouse door
and chickens flutter on the edge of my memory. Sunlight slices through dimness.
Its warmth scars gray plank walls. Feed troughs and a watering can stand waiting
for long-dead birds. Odor of sun-roasted grain lingers in the floor and rises up
when we disturb the air. Traces of chicken feed dust the floor like sawdust
spread to dance. This is the crypt of my mother's memories and mine.
A sepulcher filled with boxes and blue Samsonite and old dried chicken droppings.

At fourteen, I am too old for the antique doll bed and other artifacts of my childhood,
toys covered by damp abandonment. The baby doll is gone who knows where.
A Samsonite pullman sits in the darkest corner. It is full of paper and fabric,
corpses musty and mildewing in rain and heat. A nesting place for mice and rats,
the Samsonite decomposes like an old grave box. Becky and I do our war dance
in the dust of what was before, stomping and stamping the corners of rickety floor
warding off intruders: rats and snakes and ghosts of chickens.
I crouch and twist the pullman's latches until they pop. I am only stealing what is mine.
Becky, a mercenary, reconnoiters this tomb of birds and boxes, tempted by stories
other than her own, and some common treasure we might discover.
Her courage wanes like a moon as she imagines movement in the shadows.

The mate to this suitcase is in some motel in Emporia. Daddy went there to work.
There are no houses to draw here, he says. Daddy doesn't say what's on his mind,
that Mother has gone crazy. That while she fell to pieces, we lost our house,
we lost our family, all the things that made us one. Aftershocks, I suppose.
He doesn't say, Your mother only sits on her mother's couch, gets up to eat
and to go to bed and to take her medicine. Shakes. Shakes. She always shakes.
Instead, he makes uneasy promises. Explains why I can't go with him.
So Mother and I live with Granny and Tave, Granny's spinster sister.
Tave wears size four shoes. I wear her high heels when she's not looking.
I watch television all the time. I sit inches from the screen and pinch
the vertical hold button to keep the picture steady in my fingers so it won't roll
away. The Early Show is my favorite. Today I watched God is My Co-Pilot.

Becky gets edgy thinking about snakes and rats and escaped convicts.
I pull and push hurriedly through the contents of the suitcase, searching
for Tommy's letters to Mother. They fill blue taffeta pockets in the very back.

I close my eyes and fan my fingers over envelopes that say par avion.
Pluck one from the faded pocket like a feather plucked from the skin of a ghost.
These are mother's letters but they carry coded messages for me.

Beckie finds some old jewelry, but I must concentrate on the letters, on evidence.
This is not a game. This is not shopping a rummage sale. Not for me.
One by one I smuggle letters from the henhouse. No one notices
that I bring things back. I fold the envelope in thirds. Close the exhumed coffin.

More quickly than our entry, we step out of the snaky remains of the garden
and run the last little way to Granny's kitchen. When Beckie goes home, I hide
in my room and unfold the letter. Faded fountain-blue ink inscribes yellowing
onion skin. I gather food with my eyes, taste ink with my fingers. I forage
for any real record, any proof, any sign. I listen for echoes of Mother.

GATHERING LESSONS

Think of the October woods as a universe of spreading galaxies
cast in the high brittle racks of the disrobing deciduous,
their meaty walnut planets spinning and spilling from their dying orbits.
Think of an adolescent girl, a goddess in training,
who follows her high kinswoman into the forest.
An apprentice to the numen, Octavia,
see how the younger follows the older. Both small, both searching.
Look in their eyes. Observe their backs. See the contrariety.
Here, *says the goddess presiding,* you'll need these gloves.
I don't like gloves, *says the snippy girl.* They only get in my way.

Tave had an affinity for making a home where she found herself.
Laying left-handed claim. Laying by. She could make a footstool
from juice cans, make her own brandy, lay out a fan of scraps to make
a work of art. Her tools were in her pockets and in the backs of curtains.
On laundry day, with leathered hands, she rinsed and wrung
while Maude scrubbed and fed the clothes to the ringer. Look! There!
At the old quilt. There's a glimpse of Tavie now, in her blue dress,
her red skirt, her pink apron, her green velveteen coat. She was leftover herself.
The baby child, the runt, who refused to marry her one suitor
before she could pay for a trousseau. He was in a hurry. Married someone else.
She lost love for independence, became a woman who could make anything
from what she had, what she found. She gave as much as she salvaged.
Tavie looked like an impostor: of a woman, of a child, of an Indian maiden.
So small she special-ordered her high heels from a catalog.
She put tiny dabs of food on the edge of bread and held it while she talked,
then nibbled at it and supped her saucer of coffee, paled by evaporated milk.
On cold nights before bedtime I watched in the radiant heat of the stove
as she let down the black night of her hair and brushed it slick as satin.
Next morning, she lined hairpins on the edge of the stove and rolled
hip-length hair into a rope that she tucked and fastened at the nape of her neck.
Not a rope for any man to climb. She was no Rapunzel. That's a different tale.
A product of other choices. She and Maude had their chairs by the stove,
seats at Maude's widowed table. They shared a bed head to toe,
like toothless girls, Tave cursing in her sleep.

Best take these gloves, *counsels the wiser.* No! Really. I don't want them,

says the younger as she gropes in the loam like a blind girl, plunging
her hands into the painted leaves, searching for what she doesn't know,
what will turn her hands to saffron, to amber, to rust. The woodswoman stands,
gloved hands extended and draws to her in a stream all she needs,
tugging lightly at need for want. Like all good stories there is tragedy.

The good Octavia had a breast. The breast had a mouth that one day ate at her
until nothing was left. Not even enough meat to put on the edge of bread.
But the story doesn't end there. The girl grew into a mother
who knew the forest, a woman who walked beneath the spreading cosmos
of the seasons. She had a son. When the son came of age, he took a wife.
Their house had a yard. The yard had a walnut tree.
Gather my walnuts, Mother, *he asked,* and put them in the sack to dry.
There was a quiet moment before she said, Fetch me my gloves.

OLDEST

I.

Standing at the back door, I stomp my foot
and hold the screen open as if for flies
while I call your name till my throat hurts.

II.

When I was six I snuck off down the street
to play with Hazel Laprad, who had a
big box of Barbie clothes, a Barbie car.
Soon I heard them calling—knew Mother had
a keen switch wrung free of its bright blossoms.
I left the tiny shoes and purses and
black sequined dress, ruffled at the bottom,
tiny diamond earrings.

I ran across four backyards until I
came to the German lady's pink brick house.
They came closer, calling my name louder.
I ran hard, my head down, arms working.
Arching the sand piled against the foundation,
I climbed, mindless and wild, out of range.
When the Shepherd lunged, his chain jerked him back.
Only his dog breath on my ankle and
a drop of his saliva marked me.
I ran crying to the kitchen steps. Hot
and heaving air, I stood before a locked door,
my foot coated in gold sand
but no blood.
I saw her, my mother.
She flicked the thin reed against her skirt hem.
The German lady called from her porch,
Ze little girl muzn't do dat! You hear?

III.

I push the screen open another inch
into the weight of honeysuckle air.
My grip tightens as dew hangs, waiting with me.

Lightning bugs flash yellowish green flares
in the grayness just before dark.
Where are you? I yell once more before I
break a thin reed from the forsythia.
Before I call someone to help me search.
Then, from the shaking forsythia, you
emerge, your chest puffed out triumphantly.
I'm right here, you say in a sly voice.
I've been right here all along.

A girl-turned-wife-turned-mother I knew at Lejeune
wrote to me years later that she saw melancholy
flow through me even then, while I hung clothes on the line,
my ponytail whipping in salty coastal wind.

Said she could see both currents, the one on top
that rushed forward rippling my surface with a steady flow
of levity and sonorous nurture of others.
And that other dark undertow, the sucking current
always pulling toward bottom.

What it comes down to is watching other people have families—
all my life. Since I was seven. Even people kin to me.
And me like a cat always on the wrong side of the door.
Oh, I said my prayers. Dreamed what I wanted in
Technicolor. Hid behind doors. Slammed doors when it got bad.

Over and over I prayed. Asked God to ease my envy. To send someone
who'd give me what I needed, demonstrate it without effort or
inconvenience, or demand for gratitude. But there was always a catch.

I was so busy always asking. I never listened for an answer.
Then one day I got tired and got quiet. In my silence
I heard Him whisper, "I sent you children."

SURVIVING

The night you died
I slept in a chair
for guilt that I
could sleep and then wake up
while mourning
escaped from beneath doors
floating up the hall
to wrap around me
and bind me to earth.

When they said
How does the body look?
I answered
Fine
and rounded up
too few fingers
of bourbon.

After all this time
Grief steps aside.
I face the corridor,
walk toward the light
without fear.
I turn to see you
home from the Navy
dancing to Roy Orbison.
You, already a man
and me, still a girl.
We're just dancing
in Mother's kitchen.
I spin past you
and catch your hand
just in time
moving to *Only the Lonely.*

April
weekends closest
to the tenth I hairpin
Lover's Leap, snake Route 58
up to
52, through
Vespa, Laurel Fork and
Meadows of Dan. Short of Poplar
Camp and
the Shot Tower,
a Church of God hides in
the curve, if you don't know it's there.
The small
white church bridges
the creek and takes its name.
As a child Phyllis watched out the
window.
Saw water rush
down the rock wall, mountain
to creek, baptizing the flat stone
only
inches from her
rapt face. I pierce the curve
off the narrow highway, spiral
up hill
before I lose
momentum. A graveyard
spreads into a horseshoe of lush
laurel
vowing a deep
pink communion in June.
I park
below the graves,
walk up hill to visit
my brother, share his view a while,
picnic
on tomato

sandwich and Co-Cola,
tell him about my life and my
children.
Captive,
he listens to
my stories patiently.
The mountainside across the way's
engraved
with narrow scars,
bovine pathways dotted
with Gurnseys, Jerseys, and Brown Swiss.
Shade trees
scatter across
steep pasture, and pungent
cedar line the fencerows. When air
turns cool
or gnats rise up
in warmer springs, I
crawl through
laurel hedges
to the privacy of
discarded trappings from old grief.
Weathered
remains, faded
silk funeral flowers,
chipped florist's brick, dried carnations,
baby's
breath, mums,
miniature
American flags. Ritual
performed,
I slip back through
the rich rhododendron
to headstones and foot markers now
centuries
old. My hand sweeps
Tommy's granite marker,

his sun-warmed name. He taught me to
drive these
round roads. Drop down
in rhythm. *Feel your own*
body roll. Turn before you meet
the curve.
Slow down before
you get there. Now push it!
Anticipate. Accelerate!
Pull out!
It's like making
music. Hold your center.
Feel the road wrap around the earth.
Make it
second nature
or you'll lose it. Lose it
on these curves and it's all she wrote.
I glide
down the mountain.
I am one with my white
ragtop ride, ribboning
back down to the valley fearing
nothing.

C.P.'s Outlaws versus the Martinsville Oilers.
Hot dogs and popcorn fill Friday night air
along with moths that flutter and flirt
with danger in the field lights.
Mothers ask questions of fathers
who talk to each other.
Their deep gravelly voices face the playing field—
they judge ball speed, weigh batting stance,
third baseman's charge, pitcher's windup, the balk,
short's scoop and fire to first.
They call for double plays, measure the power
of the catcher's legs, how fast his mask comes off.
Weaver, policeman, sander, insurance man,
mailman, doctor, lawyer, teacher,
foreman, yardman, fixer, preacher.
Their sons are scattered across a diamond
cupped in advertisements for WMVA, STP,
Blacky's Texaco, First Baptist Church, Red Man
Chew, Dixie Pig Pit-Cooked Bar-B-Q.
A fastball smacks the glove on third
then rockets to first—policeman to preacher.
A mother jumps on the concrete bleacher.
Claps and fidgets and does a hip walk in her seat.
She prays for a third out.

I am a girlfriend. A cheerleader. A rising senior.
I think I am listening and watching
to learn the game of baseball. If not for my boyfriend,
I would have no interest in the game.
An initiate spectator, I have not grasped
the mental energy of baseball:
telepathy between pitcher and catcher,
tension between the batter and pitcher,
pitcher and basemen, basemen and runner,
stealer and pitcher, catcher and batter.
SA-wing batter! Swing!
I only faintly appreciate the music of a hard ball

kissing the sweet spot of a wooden bat,
the dance of a runner in a pickle,
the warrior scrimmage as the third-base runner
goes for the steal and the catcher defends home.
I foolishly think I am learning baseball:
pass balls on third strikes, pop flies, fielder's choice,
fastballs, curveballs, spitballs, grease balls,
high balls, low balls, inside, outside, bunts,
line drives, foul tips, steals, the sacrifice—
sacrifice fly, sacrifice bunt, sacrifice play on the runner.
So many sacrifices.
My boyfriend's mother shares her popcorn.
I clap when she claps. Yell when she yells.
Fidget when she fidgets. Smile when she smiles.
I watch her son, the third baseman.
He rests between batters, his right hip
shoved out to be a resting place
for the back of his gloved hand.
He spits absently and watches the pitcher approach the rubber.
He is cocky. He's also cute and a good kisser.
I forgive his arrogance for love. For his sake
I watch and learn and get my mind
around what I can in the little time I have left.
Come August he'll say no to college baseball.
I'll turn in my pompoms a year early.
I'll work half-days and he'll join the Marines.
The Cards will play the Braves in a three-game series.
Our honeymoon nights will be spent in Atlanta Stadium.
Our honeymoon days will be spent dodging rhinos
in his parents' Galaxy 500 at Lion Country Safari
and riding the roller coaster at Six Flags Over Georgia—
a preview of things to come.
I will throw up whatever I eat. I will lose before I gain.
By May I'll be a mother finishing senior English
and he'll make Lance Corporal and move us to Lejeune.
Our old paths will be unrecoverable
except through our son and daughter.

Fourteen years later, I shift my attention
from the memory of a third baseman
to the shortstop-gone-catcher
who, in the hesitation of play,
pushes out his right hip to make a resting place
for the back of his gloved hand.
He spits absently and pulls his mask over his face.
A girl somewhere in the stands
writes his name over and over in her notebook.
He squats as the pitcher addresses the rubber.
I am out of my seat as he pops up.
Out of his crouch, he flings off his mask,
backs up first.
Other players' fathers nod to me,
acknowledge a job well done.
Unlike the catcher's grandmother, I am forced out
of my element. I bridge the distance
between fidgeting mothers and voyeuristic fathers.
I am chastised by the blind tournament umpire,
my ex-mother-in-law in it right alongside me.
She shares her popcorn, watches and judges
her grandson—and me. Conspires in my strategy.
I am here, in the bleachers, willing a win
across distance only a mother can fathom.

Bill leans toward her, hand on the hood, loving her with his eyes.
The woman, head down and eyes up, leans back against the Buick's ribs.
I see this picture and want to be Mae at sixteen, about to be a bride.

They are sharing something private—a joke, lust, full hearts, like minds—
not touching, yet only a hint of separation. They are savoring what is left of courtship.
I see this picture and want to be Aunt Mae at sixteen, about to be a bride.

Her hair is swept into soft round waves, a thick roll of dark hair pinned behind.
She looks up at Uncle Bill sheepishly, pleasure already on her lips
and Bill presses toward her, hand on his new Buick's hood, loving her with just his eyes.

Bill and Mae came to visit this evening. Out for a little Sunday ride.
Him with his hardening arteries and her straining against arthritis in her back and hips.
I see this picture and want to see Aunt Mae at sixteen, about to be a bride.

Bill saw her working a tobacco field and right there decided.
He offered her a new dress, but she chose the freedom of vows in her own old shift.
Bill leans toward her, hand on the Buick's hood, loving her eye to eye.

Today they move slow. Hold hands to hold up. Stop to rest. Hard to believe back
    when there was no rest to be had, he watched her old shift slide like water across
    her breasts and hips and pool at her feet.
I want to be the young girl I never knew, sheepishly urgent. Ready to be a bride.
Her handsome man leaning toward her, hand on the hood, loving her with ready eyes.

This time I took a date.
A handsome pediatrician.
My family has the idea
I could marry him.
Aunt Dixie asks
what the doctor and I did
after the dance,
hoping for
a different answer
than twenty years ago.
I tell her we left
early Sunday morning.
Drove to Shorts Creek.
Looked at headstones.
Then took the long way
back to where we started.
Dixie tells me
I'll never have
a husband,
taking my dates
to the grave.

PILGRIMAGE

Alongside Bull Mountain Road
great Uncle Edgar's maple
catches fire come October
and burns until winter
turns it to finger-like embers.

Flatlanders look out in awe,
breathless at red and rust
textured vistas that are general
as postcards to me.
No spectacle there.

I take no annual trek
on snaking scenic roads.
My pilgrimage is here
among steel girders
and prestressed walls.

My eyes close on the cusp of November.
Ignited above fading grass
blazes old Edgar's maple phoenix.
There, panoramas ashen
against one single violent beauty.

WORK

You wake up knowing you'll work.
You don't worry that circumstances will hurt

your chances to choose your labor. It seems
your choice is made. Reams

of fabric undergird your life. But fate may
lead you down a surprising path. One day

you may wake up and find you had more choices
than you knew. You leave your bed, your home, with voices

carried in your head of who you leave behind. Here
you live out your path with collective memory. Veneer

line—I worked one for three months between Lejeune
and college. After two babies. Worked to the tune

of minimum wage, ten-hour days, and culled furniture. Once I went
into the deafening grind and buzz of the machine room. My only factory stint.

Never set foot in a towel mill. But that doesn't matter.
I dream my mother's and grandmother's dreams. Dreams of clatter

and snap, of doffers and fixers, of motion. I dream thread streaming from cotton icicles
mounted on frames. Spinning dripping cones feeding hungry looms that pulse and
    ripple

as they weave. Shuttles throwing thread. Clack-thump. Clack-thump.
Humming sirens sing fiber into endless reams of cloth. Clack-thump.

Whir. Whir. Whir. Fibrous colors drape the architecture
of my sleep. Clacking and whirring lift louder and louder to rapture.

.

WHAT TRAVELS WITH US

Maudie's house hangs on my wall,
rendered free of a photograph.
Eggplant purples and
iridescent greens and blues
draw the eye to the wall behind the table.
Fluid colors of water and emotion
create the illusion of clean white clapboards
and thin blades of familiar grass.

Illuminated by sun or incandescent light
they are graceful pigments of history
that flow across the canvas
cool and comforting
to a mysterious but healing fever.

At night, cast in light from
some other room, the iridescent oils
make her house appear moonlit.
It shimmers in half shadows, a ghost
calling as if it could tell me
all it knows. As if someone might
step out of the house into the yard
and hold the hand of someone who held me.